Teach me...
SPANISH

A Musical Journey Through the Day

by
Judy Mahoney

with Mary Cronan

W9-APU-743

10 9 8 7 6 5 4
Printed in the United States of America

www.teachmetapes.com
800-456-4656

ISBN 0-934633-05-3

teach me...
TAPES
inc.

 Lo Más Que Nos Reunimos

Lo más que nos reunimos, reunimos, reunimos
Lo más que nos reunimos seremos felices
Tus amigos son mis amigos y mis amigos son tus amigos
Lo más que nos reunimos seremos felices.

¡Hola! Me llamo María.
¿Cómo se llama?

Esta es mi familia.

Mi Padre

Mi Madre

Yo

Mi hermano

Mi Gato

El se llama Mishu. El es de color gris.

Mi Perro

El se llama Coloso. El es de color negro y blanco.

Esta es mi casa. Mi casa tiene un techo rojo y un jardín con las flores amarillas.

Mi cuarto es azul . Son las siete.

¡Levántate! ¡Levántate!

 Fray Felipe

Fray Felipe, Fray Felipe, ¿Duermes tú? ¿Duermes tú?
Suenan las campanas, suenan las campanas.
¡Din Dan Don!
¡Din Dan Don!

4 CUATRO

Hoy es lunes.
¿Sabes tú los días
de la semana?

Yo me visto.
Me pongo mi camisa.
Mis Pantalones
Mis Zapatos
Mi Sombrero

Yo tomo desayuno.
Me gusta el pan
y el jugo de naranja.

 Cabeza y Hombros Piernas y Pies

Cabeza y hombros piernas y pies piernas y pies
Cabeza y hombros piernas y pies piernas y pies
Ojos orejas boca una nariz
Cabeza y hombros piernas y pies piernas y pies.

Hace mal tiempo. Está lloviendo. Yo no puedo caminar hoy.

María Tenía un Borreguito

María tenía un borreguito,
Borreguito, borreguito,
María tenía un borreguito
Blanco como nieve.
Un día la siguió
A la escuela, a la escuela,
A la escuela,
Un día la siguió
A la escuela,
Lo cual era prohibido.

Un Elefante

Dos elefantes fueron
A jugar
En una telaraña
Se alegraron tanto
Que llamaron
A los otros elefantes
A jugar.

Cuatro ...

La Bamba

Para bailar La Bamba
Para bailar La Bamba
Se necesita una poca
De gracia
Una poca de gracia y
Otra cosita
¡Arriba!

La Cucaracha

La Cucaracha
La Cucaracha
Ya no puede caminar
Porque no tiene
Porque le faltan
Patas para caminar.

Después de la escuela, nosotros manejamos el coche a la casa.

 Las Ruedas del Coche

Las ruedas del coche van dando vueltas,
Dando vueltas, dando vueltas,
Las ruedas del coche van dando vueltas,
Por todo el pueblo.

La bocina del coche suena pip pip pip,
Pip pip pip, pip pip pip,
La bocina del coche suena pip pip pip,
Por todo el pueblo.

Los niños en el coche dicen
"Vamos a almorzar, vamos a almorzar,
Vamos a almorzar"
Los niños en el coche dicen
Vamos a almorzar
Por todo el pueblo.

Es la hora del almuerzo.

 Quieto Mi Niño

Quieto mi niño no llores
Tu papá te dará unas loras
Si esas loras no cantarán
Papá te comprará una oveja
Si la oveja no da buena lana
Entonces te dará una hermana
Si tu hermana no quiere jugar
Tu papá te llevará a un lindo lugar.

Después del almuerzo tomamos una siesta.

 **Me Gusta Ir a Pasear**

Me gusta ir a pasear por la senda del cerro
Me gusta ir a pasear con mi mochila puesta atrás
Valderé, valderá, valderé, valderá, ja-ja, valderé, valderá
Con mi mochila puesta atrás.

Después de la siesta nosotros vamos al parque. Yo veo los patos. Yo canto "Me Gusta ir a Pasear" con mis amigos.

 **Jack y Jill**

Jack y Jill subieron la cuesta
Para acarrear el agua
Jack se cayó
Quebró su corona
Y Jill se vino rodando.

 Seis Patitos

Seis patitos que yo conocía
Gordos, flacos, bonitos también
Pero el patito con la pluma en su espalda
Guió a los otros con su cuac cuac cuac,
Cuac cuac cuac, cuac cuac cuac,
Guió a los otros con su cuac cuac cuac.

Yo tengo hambre. Es la hora de la comida.

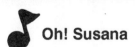 **Oh! Susana**

Yo vengo de Alabama mi banjo por mi rodilla
Me voy a Louisiana para ver a mi amor
Oh, Susana, no llores por mí
Yo vengo de Alabama mi banjo por mi rodilla.

La noche es oscura. ¿Tú ves las estrellas? Buenas noches Mamá. Buenas noches Papá. Los quiero mucho.

Buenas noches mis amigos.

 Estrellita Brillarás

Estrellita brillarás
Todo lo iluminarás
Desde aquí yo te veré
Todo el cielo azul se ve
Estrellita brillarás
Todo lo iluminarás.

El Sereno

El sereno de mi calle
Tiene una voz muy bonita
Que cuando canta las horas,
Parece una señorita
Sereno que canta, dime qué hora es
Que ha dado la una, las dos, y las tres;
Las cuatro, las cinco, las seis, las siete,
Las ocho, las nueve, las diez
Sereno que canta, dime qué hora es.

TRANSLATIONS

PAGE 1
The More We Get Together
The more we get together, together, together,
The more we get together, the happier we'll be.
For your friends are my friends
And my friends are your friends
The more we get together, the happier we'll be.

PAGE 2
Hello, my name is Marie. What is your name? This is my family. My mother, my father, my brother and me.

PAGE 3
My cat. His name is Mishu. He is grey. My dog. His name is Coloso. He is black and white. This is my house. My house has a red roof and a garden with yellow flowers.

PAGE 4
My room is blue. It is seven o'clock. Get up! Get up!

Are You Sleeping
Are you sleeping, are you sleeping?
Brother John, Brother John?
Morning bells are ringing
Morning bells are ringing
Ding, dang, dong! Ding, dang, dong!

PAGE 5
Today is Monday. Do you know the days of the week? Monday, Tuesday, Wednesday, Thursday, Friday, Saturday, Sunday.

PAGE 6
I get dressed. I put on my shirt, my pants, my shoes and my hat. I eat breakfast. I like bread and orange juice.

PAGE 7
Head, Shoulders, Knees and Toes
Head and shoulders, knees and toes, knees and toes.
Head and shoulders, knees and toes, knees and toes.
Eyes and ears and mouth and nose.
Head and shoulders, knees and toes, knees and toes.

PAGE 8
The weather is bad. It is raining. I cannot go for a walk today.

Rain, Rain, Go Away
Rain, rain, go away,
Come again another day.
Rain, rain, go away,
Little Johnny wants to play.

It's Raining, It's Pouring
It's raining, it's pouring,
The old man is snoring,
He bumped his head and went to bed
And couldn't get up in the morning.

Rainbows
Sometimes blue and sometimes green
Prettiest colors I've ever seen
Pink and purple, yellow-whee!
I love to ride those rainbows.
© Teach Me Tapes, Inc. 1985

PAGE 9
Here is my school. I say, "Good morning, Teacher." I repeat my numbers and my alphabet. One, uno; two, dos; three, tres; four, cuatro; five, cinco; six, seis; seven, siete; eight, ocho; nine, nueve; ten, diez. Yeah!
A, B, C, D, E, F, G,
H, I, J, K, L, M, N, O, P,
Q, R, S, T, U, V,
W, X, Y and Z.
Ahora sé mi abecedario. Now I know my ABCs.

PAGE 10
Mary Had a Little Lamb
Mary had a little lamb (repeat)
Its fleece was white as snow
It followed her to school one day (repeat)
Which was against the rules.

One Elephant
One elephant went out to play,
Upon a spider's web one day.
He had such enormous fun, that
He called for another elephant to come.

Two ... (repeat)
Three ... (repeat)
Four ... (repeat)
All ... (repeat)

La Bamba
To dance the bamba,
To dance the bamba,
A little grace is needed,
A little grace plus a little bit of go.

La Cucaracha
La cucaracha, la cucaracha,
Running up and down the wall
La cucaracha, la cucaracha,
Me, I have no legs at all.

PAGE 11
After school, we drive in our car to our house.

The Wheels on the Car
The wheels on the car go round and round,
Round and round, round and round,
The wheels on the car go round and round,
All around the town.

The horn on the car goes beep beep beep,
Beep beep beep, beep beep beep,
The horn on the car goes beep beep beep,
All around the town.

The children in the car say, "Let's have lunch,"
"Let's have lunch, let's have lunch,"
The children in the car say, "Let's have lunch,"
All around the town.

PAGE 12
Lunch Dialogue
Hermano: Hermana, ¿qué vamos a comer?
María: Vamos a comer tortillas con frijoles. Toma.
¿Está bien? Yo voy a probar.
Hermano: Pasa la sal.
María: Toma. Falta sal.
Hermano: Gracias.
María: ¿Quieres más frijoles?
Hermano: No, gracias.
María: Mmm ... ¡Muy ricas tortillas! ¡Gracias, Mamá!

Brother: Sister, what are we going to eat?
Marie: We're going to eat tortillas with beans. Have some. Is it OK? I'm going to try some.
Brother: Pass the salt.
Marie: Here. It's missing salt.
Brother: Thank you.
Marie: Do you want more beans?
Brother: No, thank you.
Marie: Mmm...The tortillas are very good! Thanks, Mom!

It is lunch time. After lunch, we take a nap.

Hush Little Baby
Hush little baby don't say a word,
Papa's going to buy you a mockingbird;
If that mockingbird won't sing,
Papa's going to buy you a diamond ring.
If that diamond ring turns brass,
Papa's going to buy you a looking glass;
If that looking glass falls down,
You'll still be the sweetest little baby in town.
Note: Spanish words fit music, not the English translation.

PAGE 13
After our naps, we go to the park. I see the ducks. I sing, "I Love to Go a Wandering," with my friends.

I Love to Go a Wandering
I love to go a wandering
Along the mountain path
I love to go a wandering
My knapsack on my back.
Valdore, valdora, valdore, valdora, ha-ha
Valdore, valdora
My knapsack on my back.

Jack and Jill
Jack and Jill went up the hill
To fetch a pail of water
Jack fell down and broke his crown
And Jill came tumbling after.

Six Little Ducks
Six little ducks that I once knew,
Fat ones, skinny ones, fair ones too.
But the one little duck
With the feather on his back,

He led the others with his
Quack, quack, quack,
Quack, quack, quack,
Quack, quack, quack.
He led the others with his
Quack, quack, quack.

PAGE 14
I am hungry. It is dinner time.

Oh! Susanna
Well, I come from Alabama
With a banjo on my knee,
I'm going to Louisiana, my true love for to see.
Oh, Susanna, won't you cry for me.
'Cause I come from Alabama
With a banjo on my knee.

PAGE 15
The night is dark. Do you see the stars?

Twinkle, Twinkle
Twinkle, twinkle, little star,
How I wonder what you are.
Up above the world so high,
Like a diamond in the sky,
Twinkle, twinkle, little star,
How I wonder what you are!

El Sereno
The night watchman of my street
Has a very nice voice
When he sings the hours
He sounds like a woman.
Night watchman that sings
Tell me what time it is
He has announced one o'clock
Two, three, four, five, six, seven,
Eight, nine, ten.
Night watchman who sings
Tell me what time it is.

PAGE 15
Good night, Mommy. Good night, Daddy. I love you.

Good Night, My Friends
Good night, my friends, good night
Good night, my friends, good night
Good night, my friends,
Good night, my friends,
Good night, my friends, good night

Good night!

Note: The Spanish language respects the content of the English traditional songs, therefore, this is not a word-for-word literal translation due to the different structure of the languages.

NOTES

NOTES